The Science *of* Cooking

Lara Whitehead

PM Plus

Sapphire Nonfiction

U.S. Edition © 2003 Harcourt Achieve Inc.
10801 N. MoPac Expressway
Building #3
Austin, TX 78759
www.harcourtachieve.com

Text © 2003 Cengage Learning Australia Pty Limited
Illustrations © 2003 Cengage Learning Australia Pty Limited
Originally published in Australia by Cengage Learning Australia

6 7 8 9 10 11 12   1957   15 14 13 12
4500348382

Text: Lara Whitehead
Printed in China by 1010 Printing International Ltd

Acknowledgments

Photographs by Australian Picture Library/ Corbis/ John Hulme, p. 23 top; Getty Images/ Stone, p. 5 top; Photolibrary.com, p. 5 bottom/ Science Photo Library, pp. 22 top, 22 bottom, 24, 25 top; Stock Photos/ Masterfile, front cover top left, p. 27 right; Bill Thomas, front cover top right, front cover bottom right, pp. 4, 10-11, 12-13, 14-15, 25 bottom, 27 left.

The Science of Cooking
ISBN 978 0 75 786951 8

Contents

Chapter 1

The Art and Science of Cooking

Imagine the smell of freshly baked chocolate cake, or the whiff of chopped garlic and onion sizzling in a pan on the stove.

Now imagine the smell of sour milk in the back of the refrigerator.

Foods can smell terrific or terrible, all depending on how well they have been cooked and preserved.

Although cooking is often called an art, it is also a science. Cooking makes a chemical **reaction**, or change, occur in the food, like when a pan of raw eggs gradually turns into soft, delicious scrambled eggs. In this case, the chemical reaction occurs when the heat from the stove passes through the bottom of the pan and makes the runny raw eggs become solid. Other chemical reactions happen when a cake rises in the oven or a milk mixture freezes and becomes ice cream.

You are eating a chemical reaction when you lick an ice cream cone.

DID YOU KNOW?

These souffles rising in the oven show a chemical reaction at work. Bubbles of air inside the souffle mixture are heated by the oven. They start to rise, pulling the mixture up. After a souffle comes out of the oven, the air bubbles start to cool and the souffle slowly sinks. So, eat quickly!

Chapter 2

Cooking in History

The earliest humans didn't cook their food, they simply ate it raw. Along with uncooked fruits and nuts, they ate raw insects, fish, and meat.

At some time in early history, people learned how to make fire. This discovery meant that they could roast their meat over an open fire, which made the meat easier to chew and taste better. When pottery was invented, people used pots to boil water and cook food. They could make soups and boil eggs, meat, and vegetables.

Humans continued to use open fires to cook their food for thousands of years.

Invention of pottery in the
Middle East

Humans use fire

500,000 BC

6000 BC

Slowly fireplaces and simple stone or clay ovens were invented. This made baking possible. In some parts of the world, such as China, fuel for fires was hard to find. Because of this, the Chinese learned to cook their food very quickly. They used a round-bottomed pan called a wok. These meals were cooked over a very small, hot fire.

The Chinese also invented cast iron ovens long before any other people. They built large, hot blast furnaces using the local clay soil. These furnaces were able to heat iron ore to very high temperatures. Next, they poured the iron ore into sand molds to make the first cast iron oven.

ok invented in China	Chinese begin making cast iron ovens	Europeans begin making cast iron ovens
5 BC	**200 AD**	**1400s**

In the 18th century, oven designs began to change. The British scientist Benjamin Thompson invented a closed-top cooking range. For the first time, the cook could control the amount of air flowing through the **fire box**. This new system allowed better control of the oven temperature. But, the newly designed ovens still needed fire to make heat.

In the 19th century, people began using other sources of heat for cooking. The use of natural gas and, later, the invention of electricity, brought about the modern oven.

Gas stoves become available

1856

Electric stoves become available

1900

These new energy sources were simpler to use and control. Suddenly, it was much easier to cook things.

During the 20th century, technology advanced even more. **Microwave** ovens were invented, and by the 1970s they began to appear in family kitchens. Today there is a wide variety of appliances for cooking food.

Invention of the
microwave oven

There are many appliances that
cook food in different ways

1940

Today

Chapter 3

Heat It Up!

Cooking food creates many different chemical reactions. Most foods will change in color, texture, and smell when they are cooked. There are four ways that heat travels to the food: by **radiant heat**, microwave, **convection**, and **conduction**.

Burnt toast

Goal: to burn your toast with radiant heat!

To cook a crispy piece of burnt toast, you will need a piece of bread and a toaster.

1. Put the bread in the toaster. Push the bread down and allow it to lightly toast. You might be able to see the electric coils inside the toaster getting hot next to your bread.

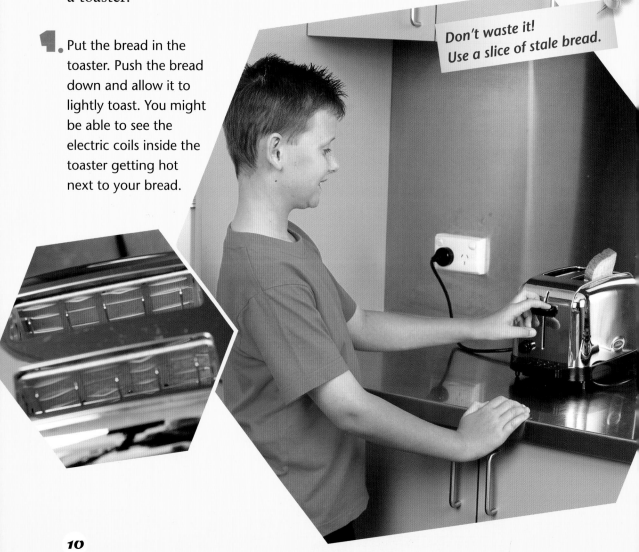

Don't waste it! Use a slice of stale bread.

2. When your bread pops up, it should be golden brown. Push it down a second time and toast again.

3. When the bread pops up this time, it should be black and nicely burnt! Your bread was near the heating coils in your toaster for just the right amount of time.

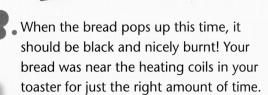

FOOD FACT

Radiant heat works by directly heating the surface of food. It doesn't cook the inside of food very well.

Rock muffins

Goal: to turn your muffin into a rock, with microwaves!

To turn a soft, moist muffin into a rock, you will need a plain muffin (without any topping or fruit fillings), a microwave-safe plate, and a microwave oven.

1. Put your muffin on the plate and into the microwave. Cook on high for 1 minute. (The time may vary according to the power of the microwave oven.)

Don't waste it! Use a stale muffin.

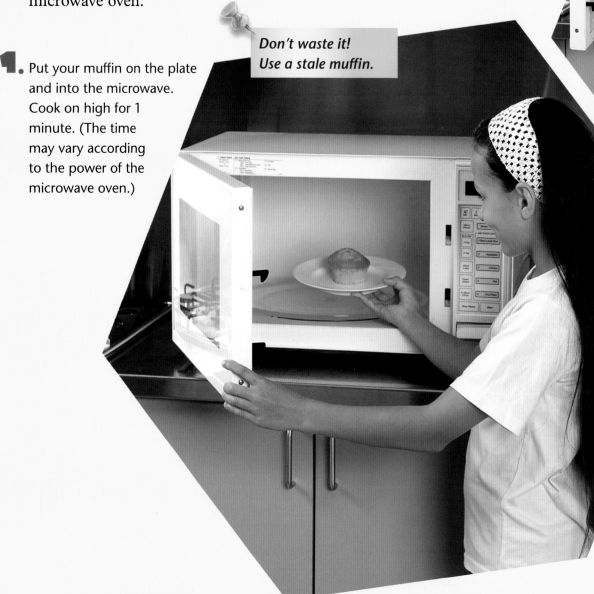

2. Carefully remove the muffin from the microwave and leave to cool for 5 minutes.

3. When cool, tap your muffin with a spoon. It should be dry and hard as a rock. You have successfully cooked away most of the moisture in your muffin!

FOOD FACT

*Microwave ovens don't create any heat. Instead, they send tiny little waves of energy into the food. The waves make the food **molecules** jump around and create heat by friction, like when you rub your hands together quickly. This friction makes the food hot.*

Green eggs

Goal: to make an egg yolk green using conduction and convection.

WARNING

Ask an adult to help you with this project.

To turn an egg green, you will need an uncooked egg, a pot, some water, and a stove top.

1. Place an egg in a pot and cover it with cold water. Put the pot on the stove and turn on the heat.

2. The heat from the gas flame will heat the bottom of the pot by conduction. The bottom of the pot will now warm the water molecules nearest to it, also by conduction.

FOOD FACT

Convection happens when heat is transferred by hot molecules of a gas (like air) or a liquid (like water). Boiling water molecules zoom around the inside of the pot. The hottest ones rise to the top. As they rise, they lose their heat and sink.

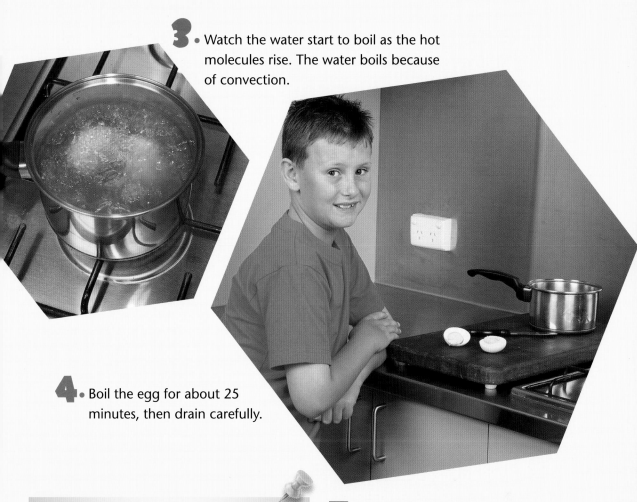

3. Watch the water start to boil as the hot molecules rise. The water boils because of convection.

4. Boil the egg for about 25 minutes, then drain carefully.

Hint: The longer the egg cooks, the more likely it is that the yolk will change color.

5. Peel the egg when it has cooled and cut the egg in half. The egg yolk should be a lovely shade of grey-green!

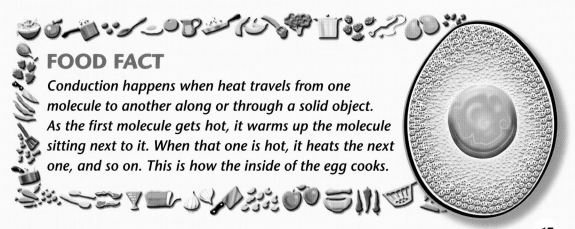

FOOD FACT

Conduction happens when heat travels from one molecule to another along or through a solid object. As the first molecule gets hot, it warms up the molecule sitting next to it. When that one is hot, it heats the next one, and so on. This is how the inside of the egg cooks.

Chapter 4

The Mystery of the Flat Bread Rolls

"Oh no ... what happened to my bread rolls? They're flat!"

Everyone in the class turned around to look at Sam Wholemeal, who was carefully taking a tray of brownish lumps out of the oven. Tonight was the annual Parents' Dinner, and Mrs. Sourdough's class was doing all of the cooking. They had been working together in the school kitchen all afternoon.

"Uhh, Sam," said Mrs. Sourdough. "Your bread rolls look rather odd. Are you sure you added all of the ingredients?"

Sam looked down at his rolls. Instead of being tall and puffy like the other ones from the Bread Team, his looked small, hard, and flat. *Not good*, he thought.

"I followed the recipe," replied Sam uncertainly. "Look, all of the ingredients are still on the table."

On the table where the Bread Team had been working were a large bag of flour, an empty milk carton, some butter, sugar, salt, a jar of dried yeast, and a glass measuring cup they had used for the water.

"We all read the recipe together, like you said to," said Sam. "And I just added the same ingredients into my bowl as the rest of the team. I even waited until last to get the warm water from the sink."

"Hmm. But your rolls don't seem to have risen," said Mrs. Sourdough, puzzled. "Are you certain you added the yeast?"

"Yes, he must have," a loud voice answered. Marsha Rye was standing next to Sam. She pointed at his hands. A few grains of yeast were still sticking to his fingers.

"Good clue, Marsha," said Mrs. Sourdough. "Sam must have used the yeast. But if the yeast was in the dough, and he added the flour and warm water, why didn't his rolls rise? We need to investigate this some more."

The other students nodded their heads and looked around the room.

Marsha walked over to the sink and turned on the hot water. The water ran cold for several seconds, then slowly started to warm up. Marsha let the water run a bit longer, wondering if Sam had done something different with his water. Suddenly the water from the faucet got very hot. Marsha jumped back and turned it off.

"I know what happened!" declared Marsha, excitedly. "Sam did add all of the ingredients, but then ... he killed his yeast!"

"Oh no," groaned Sam. "I'm not going to like this."

So, why does Marsha think Sam killed his yeast? Turn the page for the answers.

"How can I kill something that's not even alive?" grumbled Sam, flicking the last of the yeast grains off his fingers.

"Well, it's not alive in the jar," Marsha explained. "But it is a living **organism**. It's just **dormant** in the jar. You were supposed to bring it back to life by giving it some food, which was the sugar, and some moisture and warmth, which was from the water. Only you added water that was TOO HOT! You were the last person at the sink, and the water wasn't just warm any more … it was really hot. The hot water killed the yeast when you poured it in!"

"Ahh," said Mrs. Sourdough. "I think we've found the answer to our mystery."

"Yeah, well, I don't think we should serve these to the parents," said Sam, tossing one of the brown lumps up and down. "I don't want to kill anything else today!"

Chapter 5

Yeasty Beasties

A speck of dried yeast may look like a tiny grain of sand, but it is actually a living, single-celled organism. When yeast is put in warm water it "wakes up" and starts eating and multiplying. Water that is too hot will quickly kill yeast.

Sugar is yeast's favorite food. As the yeast eats the sugar, it gives off **alcohol** and **carbon dioxide** gas. This is a chemical reaction called **fermentation**.

FOOD FACT

The alcohol given off by the yeast during fermentation gives bread its special smell and flavor. The alcohol itself is cooked away by the heat from the oven.

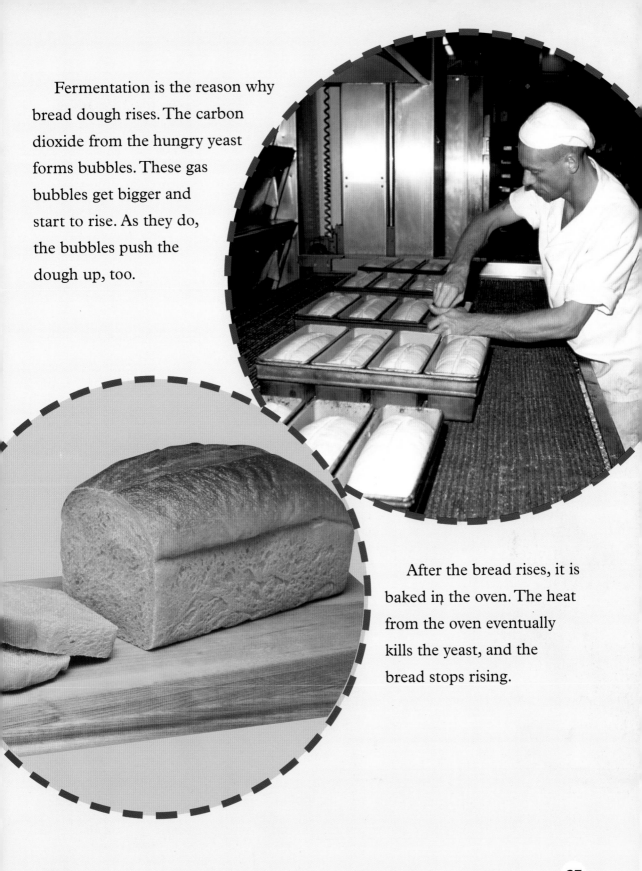

Fermentation is the reason why bread dough rises. The carbon dioxide from the hungry yeast forms bubbles. These gas bubbles get bigger and start to rise. As they do, the bubbles push the dough up, too.

After the bread rises, it is baked in the oven. The heat from the oven eventually kills the yeast, and the bread stops rising.

Chapter 6

Beware, the Lurking Bacteria

Smelly dishcloths and spoiled dinners

Have you ever found a black, squishy banana left in your school bag, or fuzz sprouting from some dinner leftovers in the refrigerator? These foods have spoiled. Spoilage is a natural process caused by **mold** and **bacteria**.

Bacteria are all around us: in the air, the soil, on our skin, and in our food. Some bacteria cause food to **rot**, and some types cause food poisoning.

Bacteria love to grow in warm, moist places, like in raw meat left at room temperature, and in used, damp dishcloths. The smell of an old dishcloth is the bacteria at work!

Your hands also carry lots of bacteria. Washing your hands before cooking and eating is a good way to avoid spreading bacteria to your food.

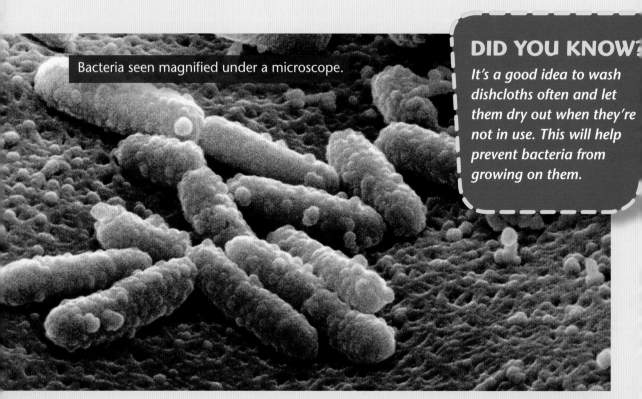

Bacteria seen magnified under a microscope.

DID YOU KNOW?

It's a good idea to wash dishcloths often and let them dry out when they're not in use. This will help prevent bacteria from growing on them.

Rotten foods

Greenish-black slime lies at the bottom of the fridge. It used to be crispy lettuce leaves. The leaves are rotting because the amount of bacteria on them has multiplied. Bacteria can also make milk go sour and meat smell. These reactions can be slowed by keeping food cold in the refrigerator or freezer.

Most food that has started to rot will look, smell, or taste bad. However, it's rare that these bacteria give people food poisoning.

FOOD FACT

Not all food bacteria are bad. Some make our food taste better, like the bacteria used to make yogurt and cheese.

YOGURT

Food poisoning

The kinds of bacteria that will make you sick are nearly invisible and grow very quickly. Food that has grown this kind of bacteria generally looks and smells fine, but it could be unsafe to eat.

Favorite places where food poisoning bacteria lurk are:

+ on raw chicken and meat

+ in cooked foods that have been out of the refrigerator for more than 2 hours

+ on unwashed cutting boards and knives

+ on unwashed hands, especially after coughing, sneezing, or using the toilet

+ in damp, dirty dishcloths and sponges

+ under your fingernails, especially after patting a cat or dog

Symptoms of food poisoning may include mild to severe diarrhea, vomiting, and intense stomach ache.

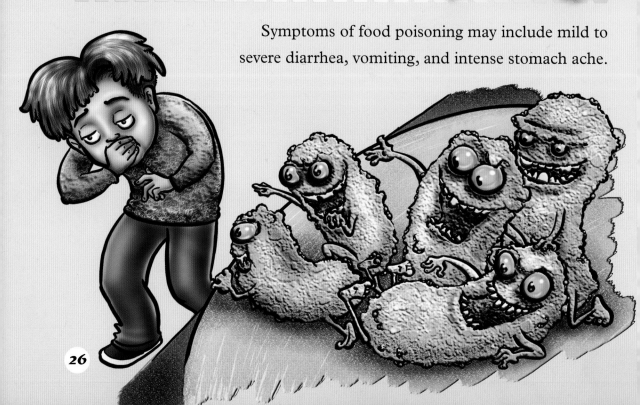

So, how do you know if your hamburger is toxic?

You can't tell just by looking at it. The only way you can really find out is by testing it in a laboratory. What you can do to prevent food poisoning is buy fresh food, and store and cook it properly. This way the bacteria won't have a chance to grow.

When you go shopping, watch out for foods that might have been contaminated.

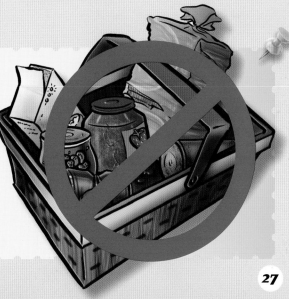

Don't buy:

+ cans that have dents, leaks, rust, or bulges

+ jars that are cracked or have loose lids

+ food with torn wrappers or packaging

27

Chapter 7

Notes from a Health Inspector

Health Inspection Report

Name: Rocking Ralph's Restaurant
Address: 129 Cook Street, Foodville

Check for:	Score	Comments
Refrigerator temp 40°F	Poor	Refrigerators unplugged!
General cleanliness	Poor	Floors and all kitchen equipment very dirty and greasy; pots and pans stacked on the floor; piles of dirty dishrags.
Covered garbage bin	Poor	Overflowing, rotten food, could attract rats!
Hot water for dishwasher	Poor	Using COLD water, no detergent; washed dishes still not clean, lipstick still on glasses.
Chemicals kept separately	Poor	Open paint tins and paint thinner on cooking bench; box of rat poison next to dry food on shelves!
Food handling	Poor	Deliveries of meat and fish left sitting near back door; raw chicken sitting on bench top.
Pests or Animals present	Poor	Flies in the kitchen; cat on bench top; dog underneath table.
Employees neat and clean	Poor	Long hair not tied up or covered; dirty aprons.

Final Score: FAIL!

Recommendations: Rocking Ralph's Restaurant breaks every rule in the book!

MUST BE CLOSED IMMEDIATELY!

"Dear Abbey"

Dear Abbey,

I'm a 12-year-old girl, and I want to know what it is like to be a vegetarian.

My older brother says that vegetarians are always sick and stop growing because they don't get enough vitamins and minerals. My mother says it's too much work and probably not a good idea. I think eating fruit and vegetables all the time would be really healthy and easy. Help! Who's right?!

Sincerely,

Celery Lover

Dear Celery Lover,

Thanks for your letter. You can tell your older brother that he is mistaken — people don't actually need meat to stay healthy. Meat does give our bodies lots of protein, vitamins, and minerals, but you can get them from non-meat foods, too.

Everyone needs to eat a variety of foods if they want to be healthy. Have a look at the food pyramid to see what I mean. Being a vegetarian doesn't mean just eating fruit and vegetables. You'll still need to eat foods from each of the food groups, which include lots of rice, beans and lentils, as well as fruits, leafy green vegetables, whole grain bread, nuts, and seeds.

You also need to be sure you're getting enough calcium, which your bones need to grow. Drink milk and eat some cheese or yogurt every day. Many vegetarians feel that they stay healthier than other people because they eat so many fresh fruits and vegetables. This gives them plenty of vitamins and minerals, which help prevent illnesses.

You might like to borrow a vegetarian cookbook from the library. I'll bet that you'll find meals your whole family will like. It won't be simple to become a vegetarian, but being willing to help plan and cook your vegetarian meals will make it easier.

Good luck!

Abbey

Glossary

alcohol   a colorless liquid produced by yeast fermentation

bacteria   single-celled organisms that often cause illness

carbon dioxide   a colorless, odorless gas found in nature

conduction   the transfer of heat from one molecule to another along or through a solid object

convection   the transfer of heat by a gas or liquid, due to the colder parts sinking and the hotter parts rising

dormant   a state similar to deep sleep

fermentation   the breakdown of sugars into alcohol and carbon dioxide

fire box   the part of a stove where the fire is built

microwave   tiny wave of energy, similar to a radio wave

molecules   the tiniest bits of a substance before it is broken down into its separate elements

mold   a soft, green growth often found on food that is spoiling

organism   a living thing

radiant heat   heat that comes directly from a heat source, such as fire

reaction   a change caused when something affects something else

rot   to go bad, break down, or decay

Index

27
26
27
28
29
30

The Science of Cooking

Have you ever made a cake or boiled an egg or wondered how cooking works? Read the history of cooking, from ancient times to today's kitchen. Conduct some experiments using different cooking methods. Find out if it's possible to kill yeast! Learn about foods the body needs to be healthy, and how to avoid the lurking bacteria that can spoil food and make you sick. There's a lot to discover about **The Science of Cooking**.

SCIENCE *in Everyday Life*

RIGBY
PM
Plus

ISBN 0-7578-6951-

9 780757 869518

ISBN 0 7578 6951 3